WAL … NE

near NORTHAMPTON

Number Fourteen in the popular series of walking guides

Contents

Walked, Written and Drawn by Clive Brown

Published by Clive Brown
ISBN 978-1-907669-14-9

PLEASE
Take care of the countryside
Your leisure is someone's livelihood

Close gates
Start no fires
Keep away from livestock and animals
Do not stray from marked paths
Take litter home
Do not damage walls, hedgerows or fences
Cross only at stiles or gates
Protect plants, trees and wildlife
Keep dogs on leads
Respect crops, machinery and rural property
Do not contaminate water

Although not essential we recommend good walking boots; during hot weather take something to drink on the way. All walks can easily be negotiated by an averagely fit person. The routes have been recently walked and surveyed, changes can however occur, please follow any signed diversions. Some paths cross fields which are under cultivation. All distances and times are approximate.

The maps give an accurate portrayal of the area, but scale has however been sacrificed in some cases for the sake of clarity and to fit restrictions of page size.

Walking Close To have taken every care in the research and production of this guide but cannot be held responsible for the safety of anyone using them.

During very wet weather, parts of these walks may become impassable through flooding, check before starting out. Stiles and rights of way can get overgrown during the summer; folding secateurs are a useful addition to a walker's rucksack.

Thanks to Angela for help in production of these booklets

Views or comments?
walkingcloseto@yahoo.co.uk

14:E

Walking Close to the Nene near Northampton

The walks contained in this booklet make use of rights of way, national recreational paths, riverside and canalside paths in the Northampton area. There is very little walking on roads except where unavoidable. Most are on firm, good quality paths and well marked and signposted. Paths may cross fields under cultivation and some are more obscure and less well directed; the detailed instructions will guide past these points. Some of the walks are in areas popular with walkers already; others are in areas less popular and perhaps less accessible.

The Nene was an important source of power before the steam age. Some of the water mills (walk nos 2 and 3) have been put to other uses, residential, retail and industrial; others are in ruins or have disappeared entirely.

A system of canals was already in place in the late 18th Century connecting the fledgling industrial areas and the major northern rivers with London via Birmingham. In 1793 the Grand Junction Canal scheme was promoted, connecting the Oxford canal at Braunston directly to London, cutting out the difficult journey on the narrow, congested route through Oxford and the unreliable passage along the Thames. The Promoters unfortunately decided they could not justify the extra costs in taking the canal through Northampton, coming only as close as Blisworth. The company however failed in its bid to tunnel through the ridge at Blisworth and the canal opened in 1796 utilising a horse drawn railway to haul freight between Stoke Bruerne and Blisworth. The tunnel was eventually completed on the second attempt in 1805 (walk nos 5 and 9). Northampton had to wait until 1815 for a connecting canal arm to be constructed between Blisworth Junction (walk nos 2 and 9) and the Nene Navigation.

Northampton missed out again in the 1830s as the London and Birmingham Railway bypassed the town, taking a fairly similar route to the canal, this time with a massive cutting at Roade (walk no 5) rather than a tunnel.

The Eleanor Cross at Hardingstone is one of three surviving crosses; one of the others is also in Northamptonshire, at Geddington. Twelve were built by Edward I at the resting places of the coffin of his wife Eleanor on its journey from Harby in Nottinghamshire, where she died, to her burial in Westminster Abbey.

Hardingstone Dyke (walk no 7) is part of the Nene flood defences; the reservoir holds 500 million gallons of flood water to alleviate flooding lower down the river.

We feel that it would be difficult to get lost with the instructions and map in this booklet, but recommend carrying an Ordnance Survey map. The walks are on Explorer Maps Nos 207,223 and 224; Landranger No. 152 covers at a smaller scale. Roads, geographical features and buildings, not on our map but visible from the walk can be easily identified

1 Sywell Wood

$6^1/_4$ Miles $2^3/_4$ Hours

Park in Mears Ashby village, no toilets, local pub the 'Griffin Arms'.

1 Start from the northwest corner of the village at the junction of Glebe Road, Earls Barton Road and North Street. From the signpost take the footpath across the open field (take the direction on the map, not the sign); this field and others on the walk may be under cultivation but paths should be well marked within any crops. Go through the trees and over the bridge, a track should be visible up the hill to the hedge and then diagonally right over the field. Cross the fence and walk down the left hand field edge to the road.

2 Continue right/straight on along the roadside path to the footpath sign, turn right through the gate and bear right to the field (the same field the walk just went through). Turn left along the field edge to the road.

3 Turn right down the roadside path, follow the road left and walk for half a mile to where the road turns sharp right. Go through the hedge gap ahead, follow the field edge left and keep on this obvious path. Turn left at the second boundary then right to get back to the original direction along the side of a very narrow field going eventually through a gate at the top right; bear left through the next gate.

4 Continue between tall trees to the left and lower trees on the right; turn right in the corner and then left through a gateway. Take a slight right to the next gateway and turn right along the field edge.

5 Turn right through the gate before the corner, start on the right hand edge and then cross to the bottom left corner and carry on down the left hand edge of the next field. Turn left past the front of derelict Hardwick Lodge and join the potholed drive through the gate. Turn right through the gate before the road is reached.

6 Go through two gates and follow the stream on the right to the corner. Carry on through the small wooden gate and the right hand side of the next field with the stream still on the right to the road and cross.

7 Continue direction next to the stream; approaching Mears Ashby keep the hedge on the right up the slope as the stream veers further away. Join the road to the right into the village and your vehicle.

14:E

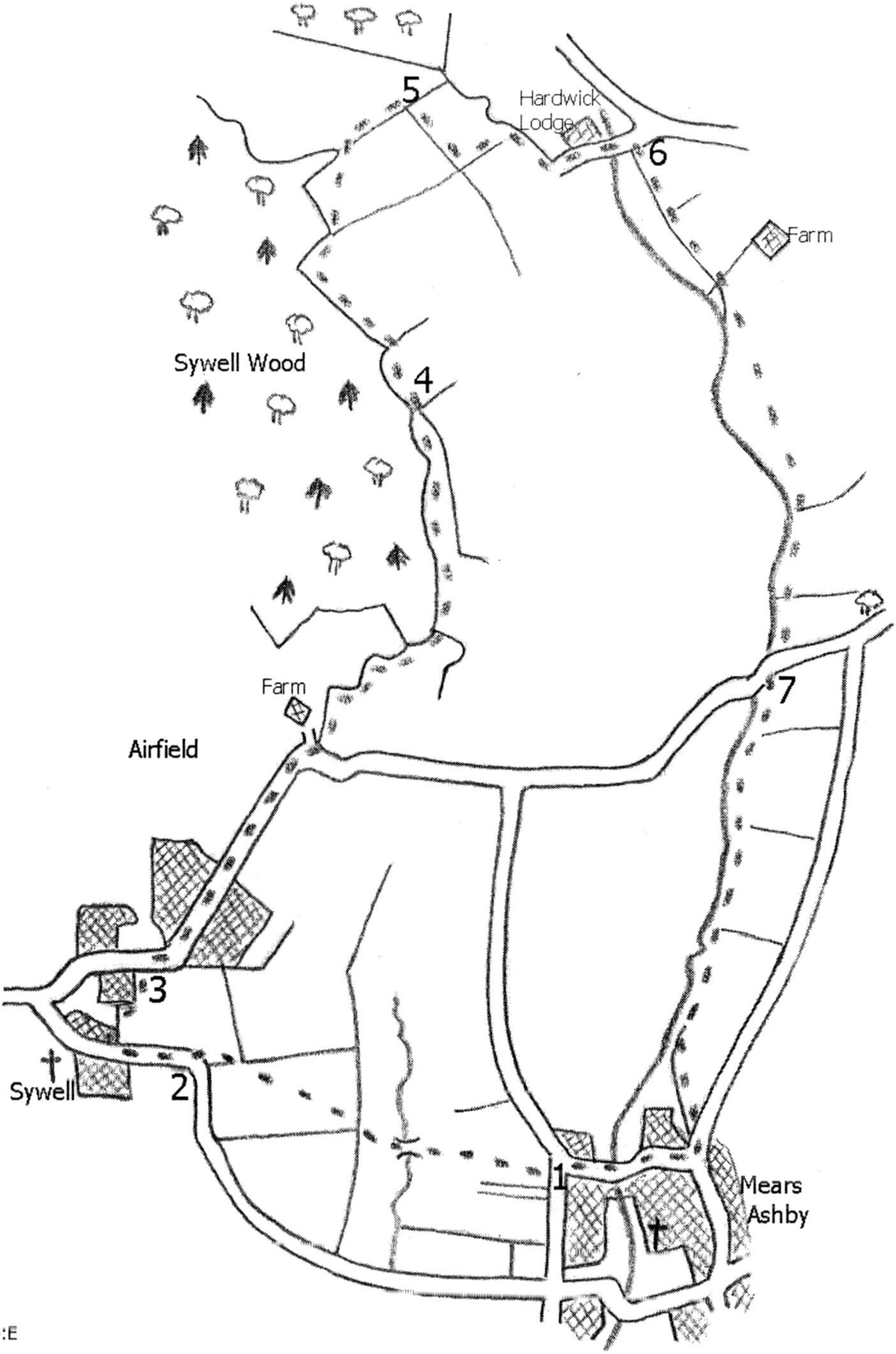
5
Hardwick
Lodge
6
Farm
Sywell Wood
4
Farm
Airfield
7
3
Sywell
2
1
Mears
Ashby

14:E

2 Duston Mill

6 Miles 3 Hours

Park in the car park close to the Nene at the end of the road past Sixfields Stadium in Northampton (A45 Weedon Road). No facilities.

1 Walk away from the car park entrance to a path coming from the left over an iron railed footbridge and turn right along the path away from the footbridge. Go over a sluice between brick walls close to some boarded up buildings, bear right then left over a brick bridge and follow this track, Duston Mill Lane to the roundabout. Turn left and cross the road at the roundabout; opposite to the left of the houses is a marker post for the Nene Way.

2 Go down this hedge lined path with the houses to the right. Cross a concrete block stile and continue along the right hand side of the field (there are Nene Way signs and markers all the way now to Kislingbury). Go through the gate on the right but maintain original direction with trees to the left, to the road.

3 Cross via the stiles, carry on through the farmyard and keep direction with the wall to the right. Pass by the narrow Bottom Spinney, as the wall stops go over an unusual wrought iron stile and footbridge. Take a left hand diagonal over this field, to the top left corner (this field and several others following may be under cultivation but tracks should be visible through any crops). Cross the stile and footbridge, follow the hedge on the left to the next stile and cross. Go directly over this field, step over the stile and bear right across the field to the road.

4 Turn left and follow the road into Kislingbury, turn left into Beech Lane, bear right and Keep going to the corner; turn left into Camp Lane a hardcore bridleway.

5 After almost exactly a half mile, just before the metal gates turn right along a rutted bridleway with grass growing in the middle. Follow the bridleway to the left, go through a gate and down the left hand side of the field; turn right with the road in the corner. Go up to the tangled remains of Pineham Barn, turn left and walk up to Bly Lane, another track.

6 Turn right, go through the gate and over a small brick arch footbridge; turn left and continue over a more substantial wooden footbridge. Turn right and follow the path with the canal on the left; approaching the bridge turn right, bear left to the gate and turn left along the road.

7 Cross the bridge and turn left along the canal towpath; continue under the A45 and past a lock. Turn left over a brick bridge and the next two more modern bridges turn right onto the car park and your vehicle.

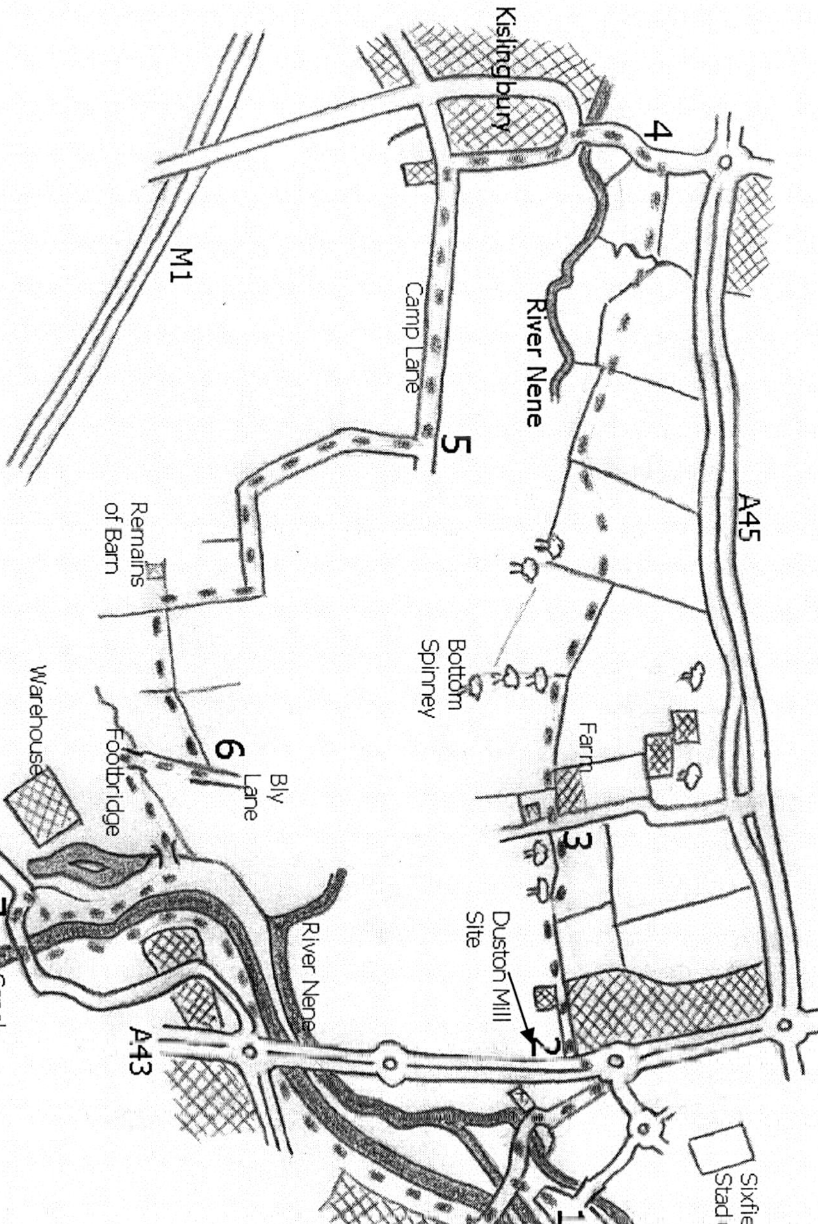
Kislingbury
4
River Nene
M1
Camp Lane
5
A45
Remains of Barn
Bottom Spinney
Farm
Warehouse
Footbridge
6
Bly Lane
3
Duston Mill Site
River Nene
7
Canal
A43
2
Sixfields Stad um
1
Park ng

14:E

3 Three Watermills

Although there isn't much left of one of them

$6^{3}/_{4}$ Miles $3^{1}/_{4}$ Hours

Park in Harpole, off the A45 east of Northampton, no toilets, two local pubs the 'Bull' (in the village) and 'Turnpike' (on the junction with the A45).

1 Walk out of Harpole towards the A45 (Northampton Road), take the footpath signed left between houses; go over the stile and down the right hand side of the left hand field. Cross the stiles and the footbridge and follow the right hand field edge to the road. Turn left along the road to the footpath sign on the right.

2 Turn right through the gate and cross the field, which may be under cultivation although the path should be well marked, at a slight diagonal to the right. At the corner bear left along the right hand field edge, keep direction with the hedges to the right and the hospital on the left, to a wide metal gate and a marker disc.

3 Turn right through a wooden gate and down the left hand field edge to the A45. Turn left, cross the road at the gap and continue ahead along Upton Lane. Go down to the bottom, bear right through the right hand gate and carry on past the front of the Upton Mill (First Watermill). Bear left through a gate and cross the iron railed bridge.

4 Bear right almost immediately and walk between the fence and the river (the lake is on the left). Continue through a gate and along Camp Lane into Kislingbury; go straight on over two junctions and turn right into Church Lane. Bear left at the 'Sun' into Mill Lane; walk past the mill (Second Watermill) and carry straight on into Willow View. Keep direction out of the village, through the kissing gate, along the field edge (wire fence to the left) and through another kissing gate to the M1.

5 Turn right, go through a gateway and bear right over the iron railed bridge and stile. Maintain direction over two stiles at the site of Harpole Mill (Third Watermill); continue over the stile/footbridge in the corner ahead and another footbridge. Keep direction, over a field which may be under cultivation, to the A45.

6 Cross this busy road carefully, take a right hand diagonal on a path which should be well marked through the first field. Keep direction across the next field and the ridges and furrows of the final field; go through the kissing gate and down the village street into Harpole and your vehicle.

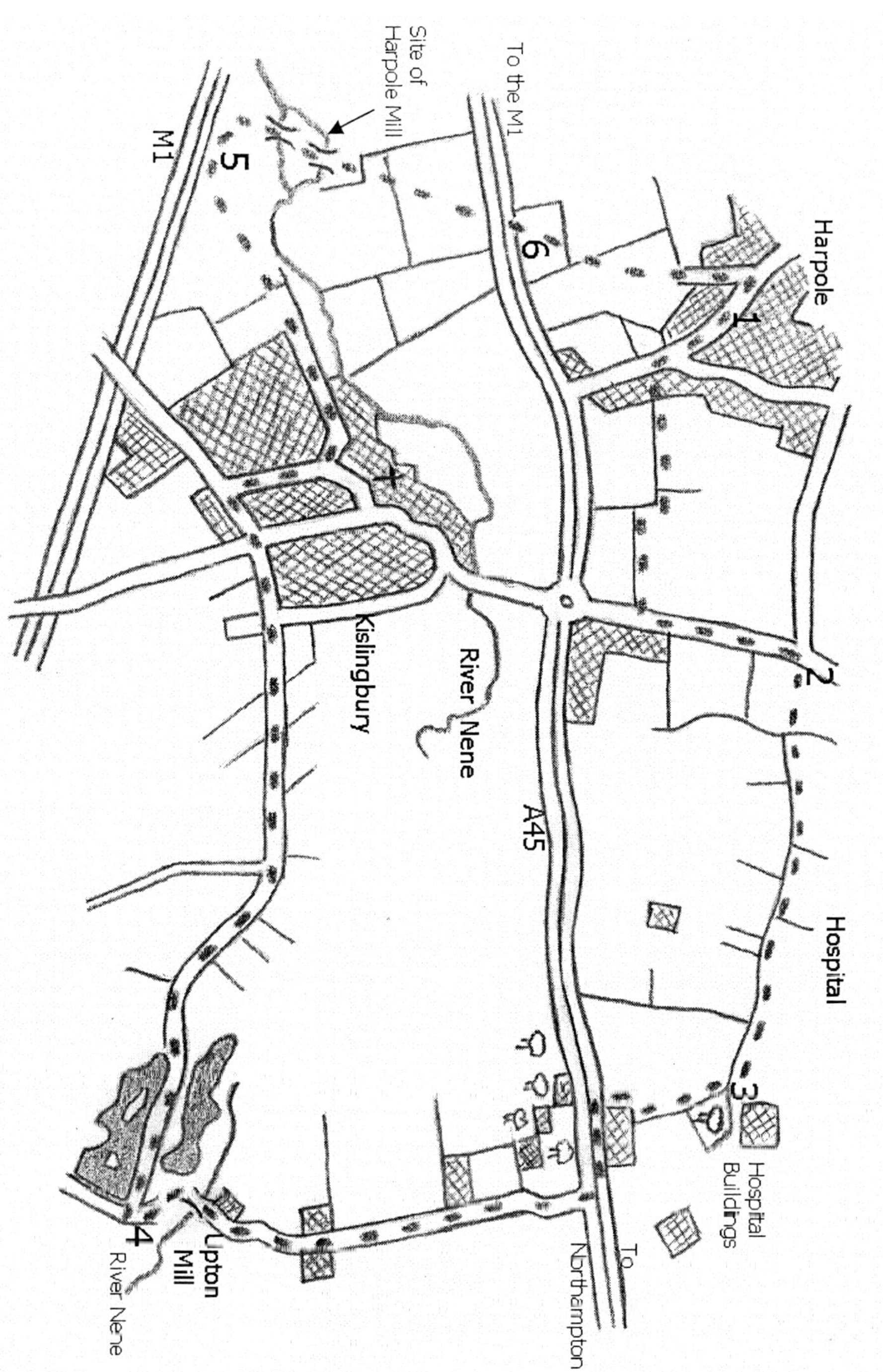
Site of
Harpole Mill
To the M1
M1
5
6
Harpole
1
Kislingbury
River Nene
A45
2
Hospital
3
Hospital
Buildings
To
Northampton
4
Upton
Mill
River Nene

4 Harlestone Heath

$7^1/_2$ Miles $3^1/_2$ Hours

Park in the wide lay-by on the side of the A428 opposite Harlestone Heath entrance. Refreshments at the adjacent garden centre.

1 Cross the road, go through the gates and down the tarmac road straight on. As this road swings left towards the Saw Mill, go straight on along a hardcore path; leave the wood past the barrier and continue down the fenced path.

2 Fork left at the junction through the concrete bollards, go under the railway and bear diagonally left over the golf course on the signposted bridle path. Walk through some trees and bear right; go through the gate and keep direction along the road into Church Brampton.

3 Turn right at the green triangle and left opposite the bridleway sign into a gravel drive (Alms Court) and bear right between fences. At the end turn right, walk up to the main road and turn left, after 100yds turn left through a gate and follow the path on a shallow diagonal right. As the path reaches a field, turn left for 40yds and then right to regain direction across the field, which may be under cultivation but a track should be well marked through any crop.

4 Turn left at the road into Jack's Lane; keep direction on the field side, over the road and across the next field. Bear left and continue along the field edge with the hedge to the left; cross a farm road and carry on along a track between two fields.

5 Go through the hedge gap and turn left, walk up to the road, go straight over, through the gate and keep direction on the farm track. Continue through the boundary and along the right hand edge of the field; carry on through a gateway, over a footbridge and under the railway. Keep going on the right hand field edge.

6 Just past the house, turn right and follow the path on the edge of the field, not the road, up to the A428. Cross, go through the gate opposite and over the field in the arrowed direction, to a stile; step over, walk around the edge of the golf course and over the grass to a corner with the church to the left.

7 Turn left through the kissing gate and down the walled path; cross over the road and continue down the gravel track to the left of the thatched house. Carry on along this track over a footbridge past a ford, bear left past a farm and go through a small gate. Walk parallel with the wall on the right, through a gate into Lower Harlestone and along a piece of road to the A428.

8 Turn right along the road to the Harlestone Heath gates and your vehicle.

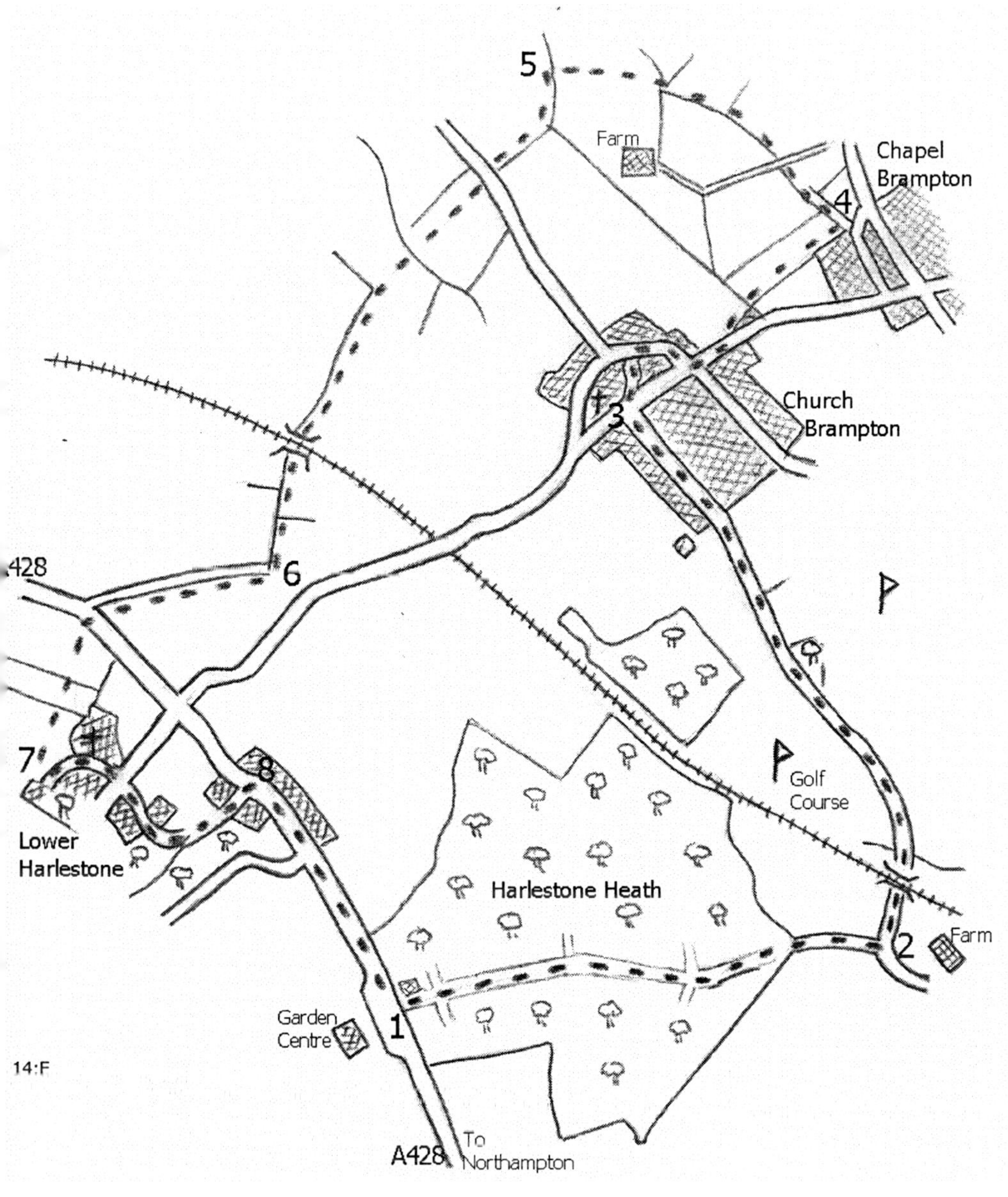

Harlestone Heath, part of the Althorp estate, is popular with walkers and dog owners; Dallington Heath to the south is unfortunately popular with joy riders, the rusty graveyard of burnt out cars is happily out of sight of these walks. The Saw Mill in the centre of the heath is the source of many of the gates and fencing on local footpaths.

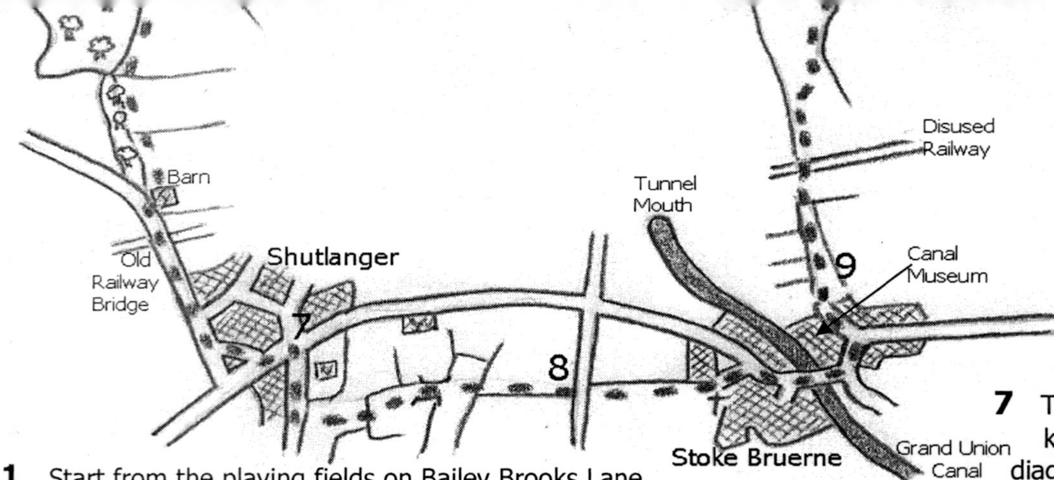

6 At the marker post in front of Nun Wood, turn left along the farm road. Carry straight on, as the road goes right, with the trees still to the right. Past the barn join the road left/ahead into Shutlanger. Turn left into Twitch Hill, go down to the road and turn left, walk up to the crossroads and turn right into Water Lane.

7 Turn left at the signpost through the kissing gate; take a slight right hand diagonal to the corner by the telegraph pole and continue with the hedge on the right to the next kissing gate. Walk to the corner, cross the footbridge and a narrow piece of open field, go through this kissing gate and follow the fence to the right.

8 Cross the road, walk up to the kissing gate, take the gate to the left of the churchyard, go down the slope with Stoke Bruerne church on the right. Turn right at the marker post and left at the signpost down the path into the village. Bear right at the T-junction past the school, cross the bridge over the canal and turn left along Mill Lane.

9 Carry on through the kissing gate, go over the stile at the end of this narrow field between the brick piers of the old bridge and cross the next stile. Take a right hand

Completion on the next Page (Fourteen)

1 Start from the playing fields on Bailey Brooks Lane, walk away from the village and carry straight on up the gravel drive (not marked as a footpath), bear left and cross the railway bridge. Continue between hedges, turn right over an easily missed stile and walk the length of the field parallel with Roade Cutting, this field may have a crop in it, but a path should be marked ready to follow, turn left at the hedge.

2 Go along the right hand field edge, bear right at the corner on to the hardcore farm road and left at a T-junction. Keep direction on the right hand edge of this narrow field to a junction of paths at a hedge gap and turn right. Cross the open field, carry on from the corner with the hedge to the left along the tree lined track.

3 Turn left at a crossroads of paths; continue on the left hand edge of the further field on the left. Turn right at the corner then left through the gap and walk down the

5 Roade Cutting

9 Miles 4½ Hours

Find a parking space in Roade Village, no toilets

14:E

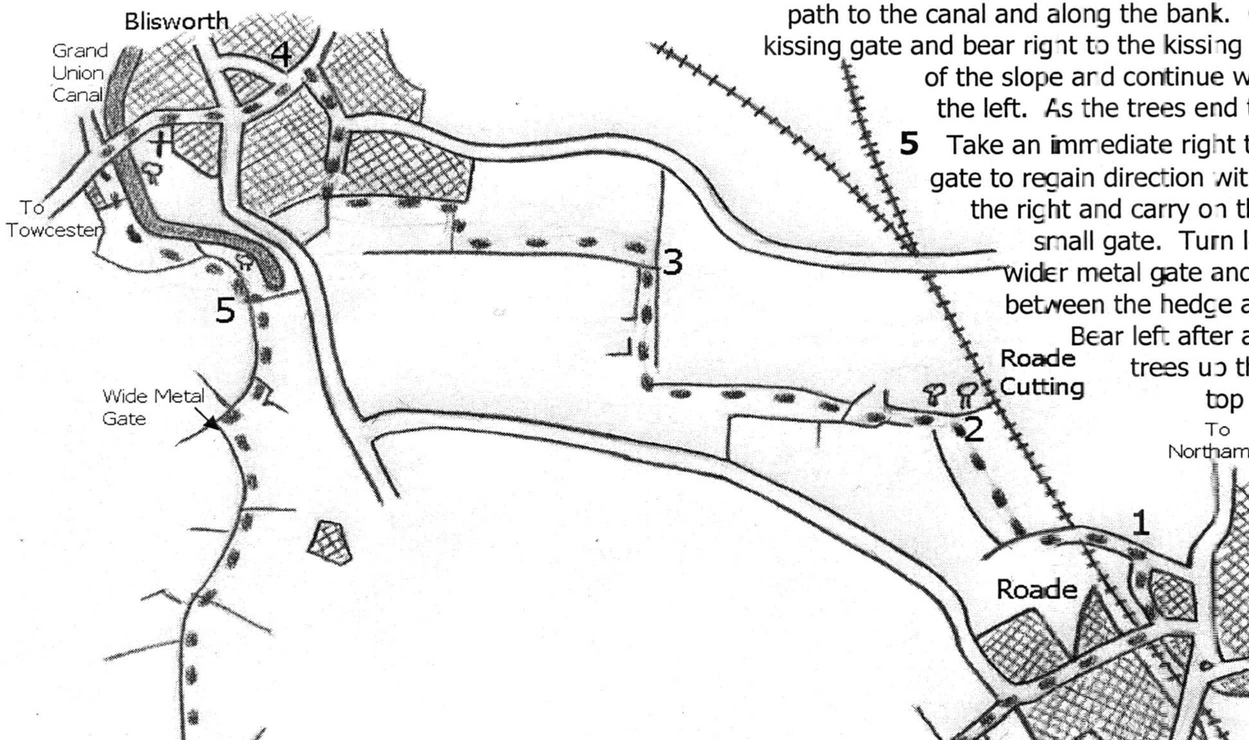

field edge parallel with the backs of the houses. Go through the gap in the corner and turn right along the fenced path into Blisworth. Carry on over the road; bear left/ahead past the school, then left almost doubling back onto High Street.

4 Keep going past the 'Royal Oak', along Towcester Road and over the canal, turn immediate left down the path to the canal and along the bank. Go through the kissing gate and bear right to the kissing gate at the top of the slope and continue with the trees to the left. As the trees end turn to the left.

5 Take an immediate right through a small gate to regain direction with the hedge on the right and carry on through another small gate. Turn left in front of a wider metal gate and keep direction between the hedge and the stream. Bear left after a small stand of trees up the slope, at the top go through the gate and turn right.

<u>Completion of 5 Roade Cutting from previous page</u>
diagonal over this field to a footbridge two thirds of the way along the right hand side. Keep going along the right hand edge of this field to a white disc marker then cross to the white disc on the other side. Follow this right hand field edge with the hedge on the right to a signpost almost hidden in the hedge.

10 Go through the hedge and turn right, follow this track along field edges as it goes right then left. Continue down the tree lined path and keep direction on the roadside path into Roade village to find your vehicle.

6 Clifford Hill

6 Miles 3 Hours

Find a parking space in Little Houghton, no toilets, local pub the 'Red Lion'

1 Start from the crossroads at the church. Walk down Lodge Road, opposite the church to the end, through the gate and over the A428. Go through the gate ahead and along the tarmac road for half a mile to a signpost; turn left through a green metal gate and walk down the right hand side of the field. Cross the footbridge turn right along the right hand side of this field to the boundary and turn left at the marker post. Follow the left hand side of the field to the hedge gap and go through.

2 Turn right along the old section of road to the A428 at Brafield-on–the-Green, cross and walk ahead down Billing Road. Turn right at the tarmac path signposted bridleway, fork right at the marker post past the front of the 'Red Lion' along Bridle Path and past the end of Chapel Lane. Bear left then right to the T-junction.

3 Turn left and fork right past the green and the pond. Carry on through the gate at the end; go straight on at the signpost (actually slightly to the right) along the left hand side of the field, hedge to the left. Go through the metal gate and continue on the left hand side of the field to the T-junction of paths.

4 Turn left signposted Cogenhoe, follow the left hand side of the field and branch to the left under the power lines. Go over a footbridge, past the pocket park and bear left uphill through a gate to the 'Royal Oak' on Station Road in Cogenhoe.

5 Turn left through the village on Station Road to the T-junction at the bottom of the hill and turn right. Walk up to the stile on the left just before the bridge.

6 Step over and turn right; follow the wall to the river and turn left along the bank. Cross over at the concrete footbridge and the lock; turn left and go over the next footbridge. Continue along the bank with the river to the left to the Clifford Hill lock and cross over the river.

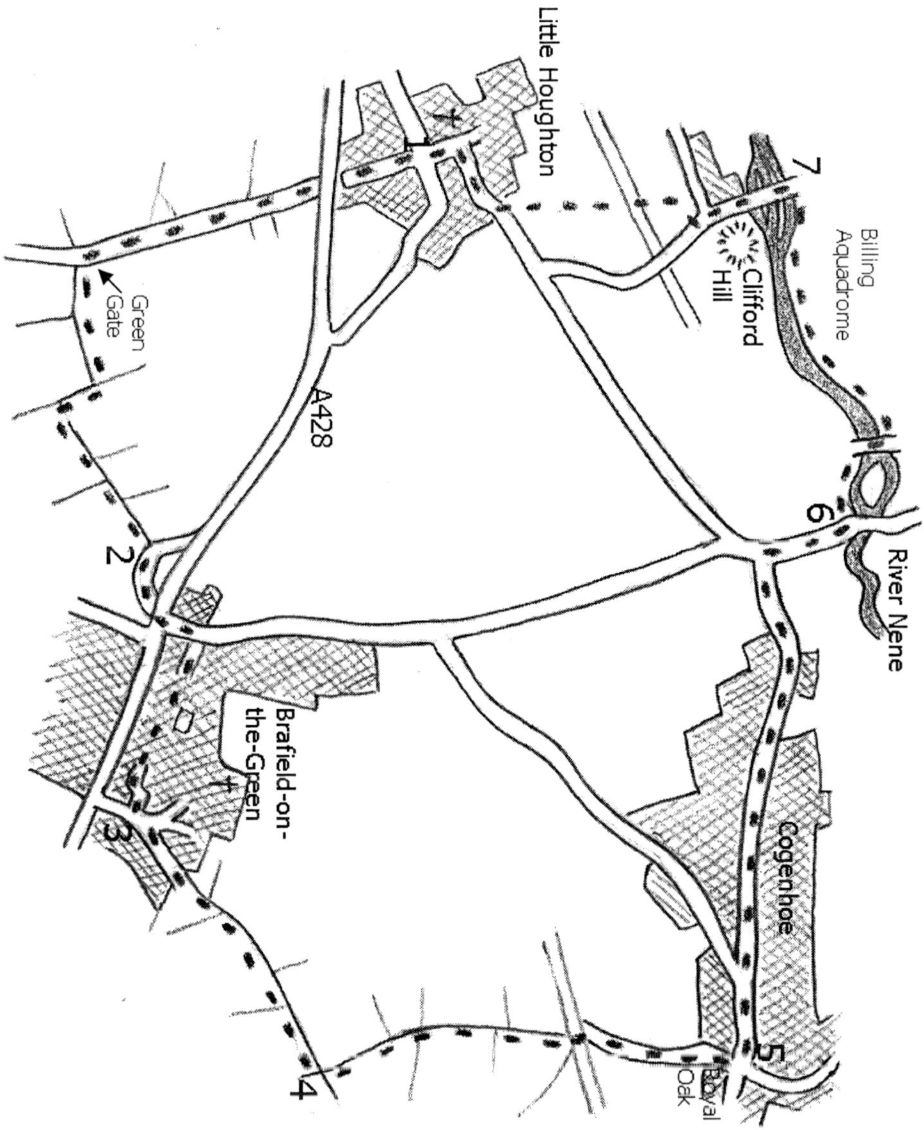

7 Carry in along the road between the old mill and Clifford Hill, turn right at the signpost through the V-stile and across the field to the right of the pylon, the track should be visible through any crop. Cross the disused railway line, go through the gate and up and over the hill. Pass through the kissing gate in the corner, turn right and follow the road into Little Houghton and your vehicle.

14:E

7 Hardingstone Dyke

7 Miles $3^1/_4$ Hours

Find a parking space in Little Houghton, no toilets, local pub the 'Red Lion'

1 Start from the church gate, facing away from the church turn left then left at the crossroads, signposted Cogenhoe. Walk down to the corner and turn right into Station Road. Just past where the houses stop turn left through the kissing gate and follow the arrowed direction over the field, this field may have a crop in it but a track should be well marked. At the bottom of the slope go through the gate and over the old railway line; cross the next field and go through the V-stile.

2 Bear left; walk through the gates and between Clifford Hill and the Mill House to the lock. Cross the river and turn left after the lock (don't go over the third bridge). Continue over the long railed footbridge over the weir and along the tree lined riverbank. Turn right with the trees away from the river with the dyke on the left.

3 Cross the stile, turn left over the bridge and left again over the stile next to the green metal gate; continue down the tarmac road. At the next, high, green gate turn right and walk between high wire fences to the lock. Cross and bear right, through the gate and up the steps past the brick hut to the top of the bank.

4 Turn left over the concrete walkway, go left along the bank; follow as it swings gently right. As the curve straightens out go through the gate onto Hardingstone Dyke, turn left at the next gate, cross the bridge and go through the kissing gate. Take a right hand diagonal, crossing a footbridge/stile midway to the A428.

5 Go a short way right, then left into Great Houghton; keep direction along the High Street, just after the village sign turn left down the signposted fenced path. Bear left between houses, then right down the side of the play area; go straight over the field ahead (a track should be visible within any crop) and cross the stile. Follow the left hand field edge and turn left over a concrete ladder stile.

6 Cross the old railway line and turn right after the stile; cut the corner to a double stile and follow the right hand field edge to green metal gates either side of a tarmac farm road. Go through both gates and walk down the right hand side of the field ahead. Cross the footbridge in the corner, turn right along the right hand side of this field to the boundary and turn left at the marker post. Follow the left hand side of the field to the hedge gap and go through.

7 Turn right and follow the old section of road to the A428 at Brafield-on–the-green. Carry on through the village on the A428 to Church Lane and turn left.

<u>Completed on next Page (Eighteen)</u>

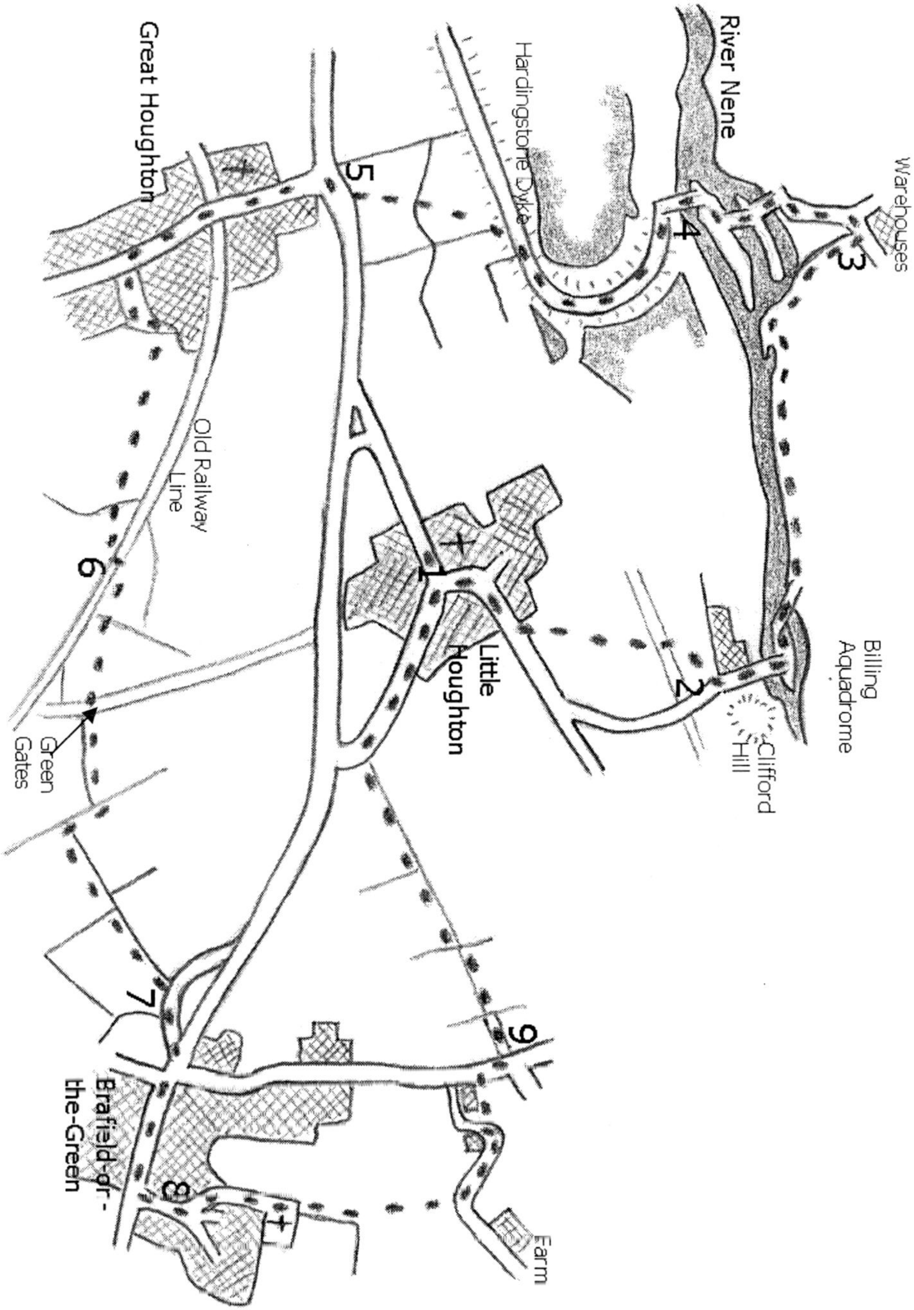
River Nene
Warehouses
3
4
Hardingstone Dyke
5
Great Houghton
Old Railway Line
6
Green Gates
7
Brafield-on-the-Green
8
Farm
9
1
Little Houghton
2
Clifford Hill
Billing Aquadrome

Completion of 7 Hardingstone Dyke from Page Sixteen

8 Fork left at the village green towards the church, continue through the churchyard and along the right hand edge of the field beyond. Bear left at the hedge corner by the marker post (not straight on) go past the telegraph poles to the left, join the farm road at its corner and turn left over the cattle grid. Follow the farm road and turn right along the back of the right hand house. Cross the stile on to the road turn right for 50yds then left at the bridleway sign.

9 Continue past the gate, bear left at the corner and regain direction on the right hand edge of the next field, go through a boundary and up to the road. Turn right and walk back into Little Houghton and your vehicle.

---

8 Commander's Spinney

3$^1/_2$ Miles 2 Hours

Park in the free car park off Broad Street (the main road through) in Earls Barton. Pubs, shops, coffee shop and takeaways all local; no toilets.

1 Turn left out of the car park entrance through The Square and along West Street. Go left at the T-junction (B573), cross the road and turn right through the gate at the footpath sign.

2 Follow the track in the arrowed direction to the right hand side of the trees ahead. Cross the stile, carry on past the trees, over the stile, through the gate and across the field beyond, this field and several others in this walk may be under cultivation but tracks should be visible through them. Cross the road, go through the hedge gap and keep direction through three kissing gates.

3 At the third kissing gate, take a right hand diagonal to the gate in the corner and go down the short road into Ecton. Turn left and follow the road out of the village and over the bridge across the A45.

4 On the other side of the bridge take an immediate left past the barrier, at the bottom of the slope turn right along the track past Commander's Spinney and continue ahead with the dyke to the right. Keep on this hardcore road across a junction, down a fenced path and over a narrow stone bridge; bear right to the lock and cross both bridges. Go up to the mill and turn left at the Nene Way signpost.

5 Walk past the side of the mill and follow the footpath along the rivers edge as it meanders all the way to Whiston Lock. Turn left over the lock and the wide bridge.

6 Go straight on away from the river, bear right and cross a high sided footbridge; continue through a small gate and take a right hand diagonal over the field to the gate, a track should be visible within any crop. Bear left up the hardcore track and cross the footbridge over the A45.

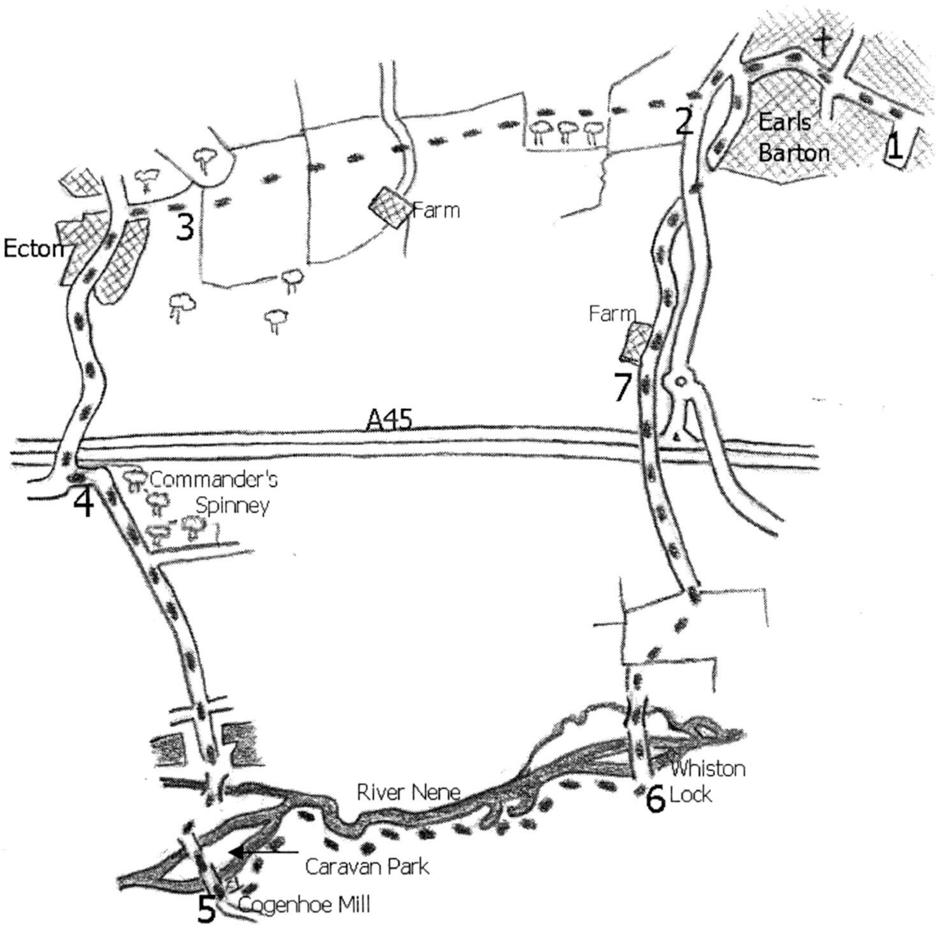

7 Keep direction past the white gate and the farm along the right of way parallel to the road; cross the road when necessary and continue up the hill. Turn right and follow West Street back into the village to the car park and your vehicle.

The striking landmark of Earls Barton church tower is one of the finest surviving examples of Saxon church architecture; it celebrated its millennium in 1970. Vikings had destroyed the previous church.

14:E

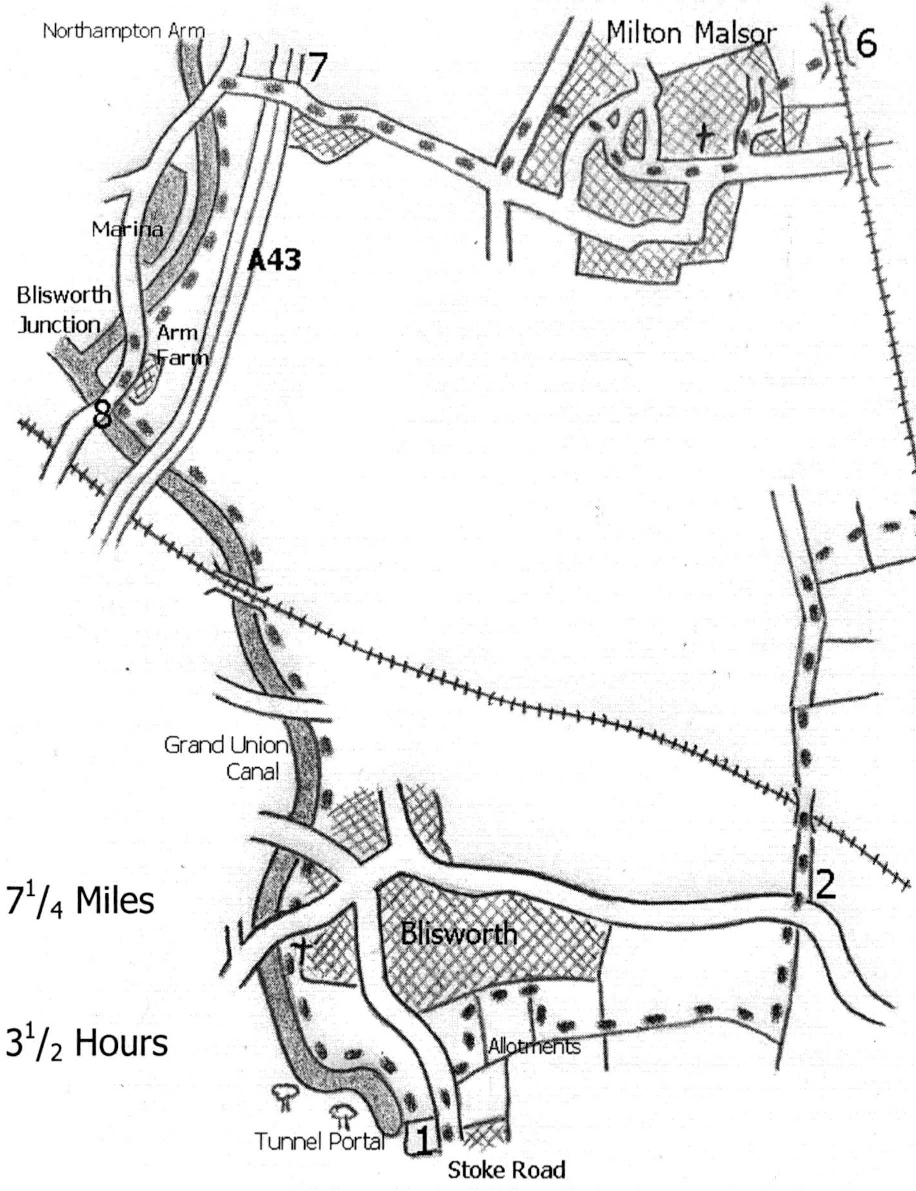

7¼ Miles

3½ Hours

9 Blisworth Junction

Park in the small area close to the mouth of Blisworth Tunnel off Stoke Road close to the Stone Works. No Toilets; pubs and other facilities in the village (half a mile).

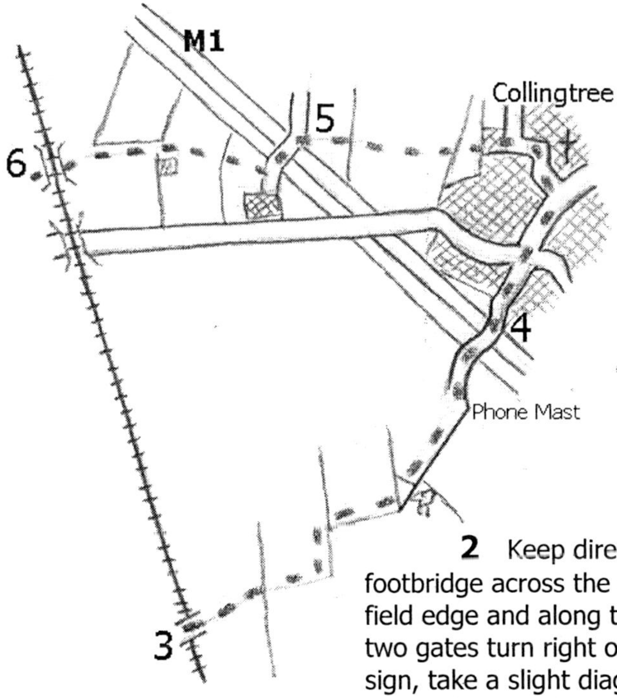

1 Go left out of the entrance along Stoke Road towards the village. Turn right at the bridleway sign into the allotments, bear right and follow the track left; turn right at the footpath sign and go along the left hand edge of the field to the boundary. Go through the gap, turn right then left in the corner and follow the right hand field edge to the top corner. Turn left and walk down to the road.

2 Keep direction over the road, the footbridge across the railway, down the left hand field edge and along the fenced farm track. After two gates turn right over the stile at the footpath sign, take a slight diagonal left to the stile at the top of the rise, then cross to the bridge and go over the railway.

3 Carry on along the left hand field edge, cross the next stile and the field beyond (there may be a crop in this field but a track should be visible through it). Turn left along the gravel farm track; follow round to the right then bear left past a small brick building. Continue past a phone mast and cross over the M1.

4 Walk into Collingtree village, go straight over the crossroads and turn left in front of the church, follow the road round and keep direction over three stiles ahead. Continue on the well marked path over a rickety stile, down a fenced track through a kissing gate and over another stile.

5 Re-cross the motorway; turn left then almost immediate right over a stile. Cross the field in the arrowed direction. Step over the stile next to the tree and walk across the field on the normally well marked track just to the right of the small brick barn. Carry on along the right hand edge of the field, bear left at the corner and go under the railway.

6 Head for the top left field corner. Go between the garages, turn left into Stockwell Way and follow it right/ahead to a T-junction. Turn right and walk into Milton Malsor past the church and the 'Compass' to the village green. Continue along the footpath signposted between the village hall and the 'Greyhound', turn left at the road walk up to the crossroads and turn right.

<u>Completed on the next Page (Twenty Two)</u>

Completion of 9 Blisworth Junction from Page Twenty One

7 Go over the bridge across the A43 dual carriageway and turn left; cross the road and descend to the towpath on the right of the bridge. Turn left and follow the canal past the marina to the next bridge. Go up to the road and turn right past Arm Farm to the bridge at Blisworth Junction.

8 Turn left and follow the canal towpath under the A43 and the railway, keep going past Blisworth village to Blisworth Tunnel portal, bear left up the ramp to the car park and your vehicle.

---

10 Nobottle Wood

5¾ Miles 2¾ Hours

Park in Harpole, off the A45 east of Northampton, no toilets, two local pubs the 'Bull' (in the village) and 'Turnpike' (on the junction with the A45).

1 Leave the village along Upper High Street, keep along this not very busy road to the T-junction and cross over.

2 Go through the gate slightly to the right and up the field edge with the hedge to the left. Carry on from the boundary with the hedge now right through the hedge gap and down a short length of left hand field edge. Pass through the gate and follow the track parallel to the hedge on the right, continue direction with the hedge now closer and bear right along the hardcore farm track to the road. Turn left and follow the road down into Harlestone village.

3 Bear left at the marker disc on the telegraph pole uphill to the Midshires Way signpost. Go through the gate and across the field, exit through the wider gate and turn left with the wall to the left, through the gate at the end. Turn right on the track up the right hand field edge with the hedge to the right and continue through the dip close to Yewtree Spinney.

4 Go through the gateway and bear right over the field ahead which may be under cultivation although a path should be well marked within any crop. Pass through the gateway by the derelict barn and bear slight right across the next field. Bear left from the next hedge gap to the corner of Nobottle Wood.

5 Bear right with the trees to the right; maintain direction through Short Wood and the right hand field edge. Pass through the gate and bear left through three narrower gates into Nobottle village. Turn right and almost immediate left down the narrow tarmac road, at the signpost turn left along the hedged path.

6 Step over the stile and walk up the sloping right hand field edge, cross the stile on the right and carry on with the hedge now left. At the top left go through the gate and over the stile, continue ahead along the farm track between the fence and the hedge to the far corner of Harpole Covert.

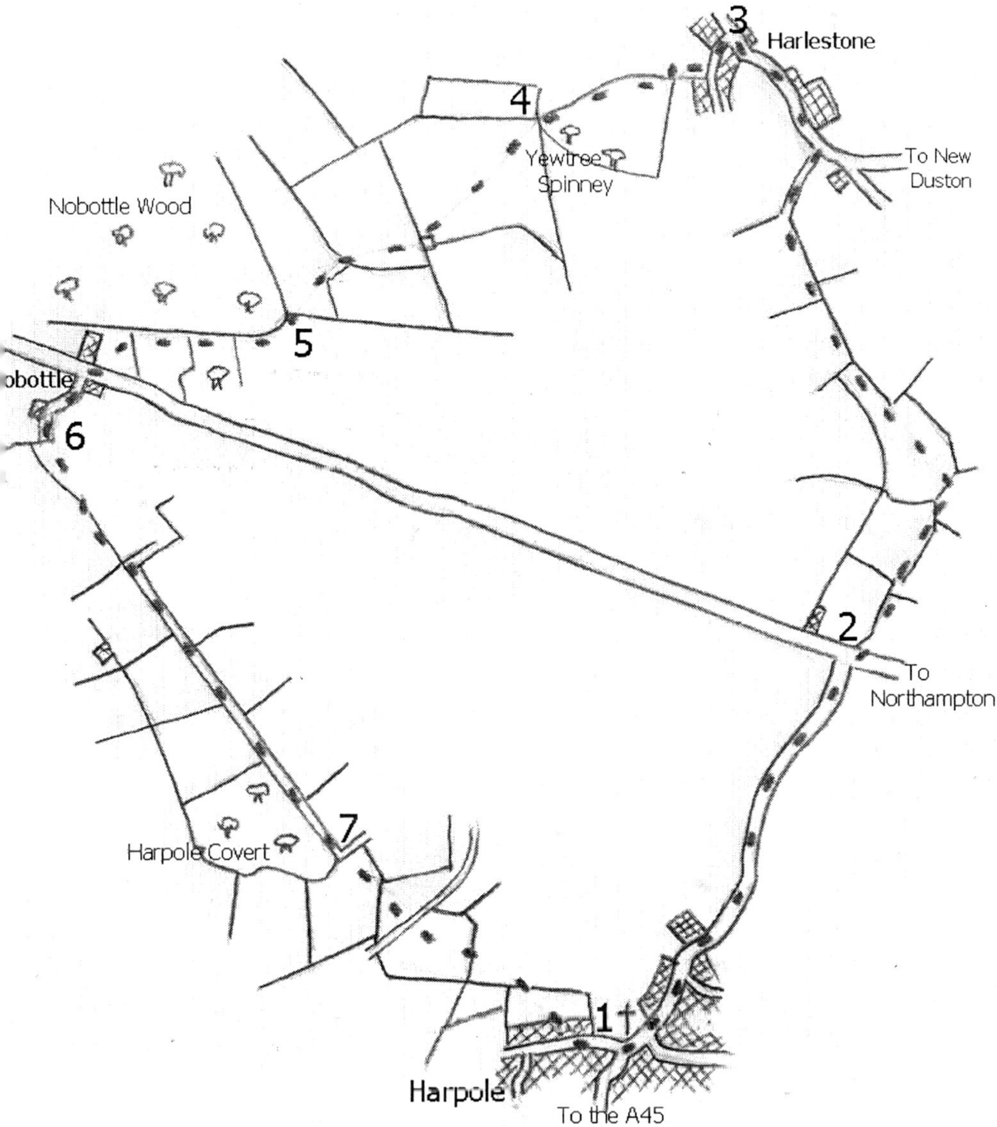

7 Cross the stile and descend the steps, go over the field (a track should be visible) and up the steps on the other side. Keep direction through kissing gates to the edge of Harpole village, bear right to School Lane and left back into the village and your vehicle.

The 'Walking Close to' Series

Peterborough
The Nene near Peterborough
The Nene Valley Railway near Wansford
The Nene near Oundle
The Torpel Way (Peterborough to Stamford)
The Great North Road near Stilton

Cambridge
Grafham Water (Huntingdonshire)
The Great Ouse in Huntingdonshire
The Cam and the Granta near Cambridge
Newmarket
The Isle of Ely

Northamptonshire/Warwickshire
The Nene near Thrapston
The Nene near Wellingborough
The River Ise near Kettering
The Nene near Northampton
Pitsford Water
Rockingham Forest
Daventry and North West Northamptonshire
Rugby

Leicestershire
Rutland Water
Eye Brook near Uppingham
The Soar near Leicester
Lutterworth
The Vale of Belvoir (North Leicestershire)
Melton Mowbray
The Welland near Market Harborough

Lincolnshire
The Welland near Stamford
Bourne and the Deepings
South Lincolnshire

Suffolk
Lavenham in Suffolk
Bury St Edmunds
The Stour near Sudbury
The Orwell near Ipswich
Dedham Vale
Stowmarket
Clare, Cavendish and Haverhill
Southwold and the Suffolk Coast

Hampshire
Romsey and the Test Valley

Essex/Hertfordshire
Hertford and the Lee Valley
The Colne near Colchester
Epping Forest (North London)
Chelmsford

Wiltshire/Bath
The Avon near Bath
Bradford-on-Avon
Corsham and Box
The Avon near Chippenham

Bedfordshire/Milton Keynes
The Great Ouse near Bedford
The Great Ouse North of Milton Keynes
Woburn Abbey

Somerset & Devon
Cheddar Gorge
Glastonbury and the City of Wells
The Quantock Hills
The East Devon Coast (Sidmouth, Branscombe and Beer)
Exmouth and East Devon

Norfolk
The Norfolk Broads (Northern Area)
The Norfolk Broads (Southern Area)
The Great Ouse near King's Lynn
North West Norfolk (Hunstanton and Wells)
Thetford Forest
North Norfolk (Cromer and Sheringham)

Nottinghamshire
Sherwood Forest
The Dukeries (Sherwood Forest)
The Trent near Nottingham

Oxfordshire/Berkshire
The Thames near Oxford
The Cotswolds near Witney
The Vale of White Horse
Woodstock and Blenheim Palace
Henley-on-Thames
Banbury
The River Pang (Reading/Newbury)
The Kennet near Newbury

Cumbria
Cartmel and Southern Lakeland

Hereford and Worcester
The Severn near Worcester
South West Herefordshire (Hay-on-Wye and Kington)
The Malvern Hills